TITANIC: Enterprise and Risk

What modern businesses can learn from the Olympic class liners, 100 years on

Kevin McPhillips

Second edition

© Kevin McPhillips 2012, 2013

Sentiamus Publishing, Linlithgow, Scotland, UK

ISBN: 978-0-9576103-0-9

Reviews of first edition

"For a book on business and project management, this is a real page-turner. The story of Titanic is so familiar and dramatic that it comes as a surprise, to read this fresh, sober perspective, focused not on the great tragedy itself, but on the people, the businesses, the institutions and the historical context that all contributed to the disaster. While weaving a classic story-telling narrative, McPhillips manages to extract those universal project management lessons, that are as applicable today as they were (or should have been) 100 years ago.

McPhillips presents the key lessons and contributing factors from this disaster, bringing focus to those elements that should be the primary concern of all project management and business professionals today." Scotinus

"In Business, icebergs are to be expected. The question is how few can you hit and how well you are prepared for their impact. Kevin uses the Titanic metaphor to tease out the strategies, tactics and awareness that business leaders need to bring to the table."
Frank Hannigan, Chairman, Razor Communications

"The level of research provides much richer pictures than what is provided on popular media and this additional detail will challenge readers to weigh up conflicts of risk and objectives in project delivery that are at the root of change management ." Peter DL

"The sign of an expert is the ability to make a subject easy to understand. McPhillips certainly does that here, helping make both a dry and difficult subject into an easy but valuable read. The enduring story of the Titanic is a good choice of backdrop to the consideration of risk in an organisation, and how decisions at all levels and times in a project's lifespan can affect it. This book would be good reading for all staff in an enterprise, and helps bring some very important points home as to the role everyone has to play." Andrew Hilton

"A fascinating read which explores, in some depth, the commercial and personal decisions (and indeed errors) taken as the Titanic story moves from concept, design, build through to sailing and to the end we all know of. The book invites the reader to consider parallels with their own business life and perhaps consider whether during the twists and turns of the inevitable focus on delivery they are falling into similar situations." Brian F

For Marian, Conor, Iona and Tara

Contents

Preface

"The perfect ship was no longer the vessel that best expressed the art of the shipbuilder. It was the ship that made the most money."

Walter Lord, The Night Lives On

In 1852, Isombard Kingdom Brunel, probably the most celebrated engineer of that century, sketched out a design for a liner, called SS Great Eastern. This was to be a purpose built passenger carrier for the growing trans-Atlantic market. Build completed in 1858, this ship was built to be profitable, but even more so, safe. His initial sketched suggested dimensions of *"Say 600 ft x 65 ft x 30 ft"*. This was ambitious, about six times larger than any ship afloat, with a capacity for 4,000 passengers. But it was a time of enterprise and vision.

SS Great Eastern's keel was laid down on 1 May 1854. She was the first ship to incorporate a double-skinned hull, a feature now compulsory for reasons of safety. The hull was all-iron, divided by two 350 ft long, 60 ft high, longitudinal bulkheads and 15 transverse bulkheads, each 30 ft above water.

☆☆☆

Titanic and her sisters were also born from a vision in competitive times. Most people involved in the creation and running of these massive liners had every right to be proud of the parts they played. However, risks were taken, and most of those who lost their lives or loved ones on Titanic's maiden voyage were unaware of those risks and consequences.

Have lessons been learned, or does history repeat? What other businesses, small or global, are driven by visions of size and a desire to push boundaries? Risk is an important part of enterprise, but do those leading their businesses consider the possibility of the worst happening, and plan to avoid it? Do we place too much trust in those at the helm, and those who wrote the rules?

This book is not intended as a detailed guide to the Titanic and its fate; that information is readily available elsewhere, and the story has been well embellished in book and film. My focus is on the business, the people who ran it, and the pressures they encountered. The book follows the structure of a business project through to its transition to business operations, and uses the story of the Olympic and Titanic to illustrate points that are still common and relevant to businesses and organisations in the twenty first century.

The parallels elsewhere are countless – consider disasters in areas such as transport, power generation and banking. By providing some background on the business decisions that led to the construction and demise of the Titanic, and to the wide reaching consequences, my hope is that you will form your own opinions on similar matters in your own domain, regardless of differences in scale. It is easy to identify causes in hindsight, but here is my main challenge – **how many problems can be prevented by being alert to the warnings all around?**

Kevin McPhillips, March 2012

A Rising Tide

*Gaining advantage in a growing market; choosing
appropriate partners; sharing a vision and uniting behind
it; setting new standards; economic and political
considerations*

The North Atlantic was a busy place in the latter half of the
nineteenth century. By the first decade of the twentieth
century, competition across the various transport lines was
fierce, but the market was growing.

Under Thomas Ismay, White Star Line had become a major
player in trans-Atlantic passenger transport, second only to
Cunard Line. His son, Bruce Ismay, had succeeded him as
managing director of White Star. Although the White Star
Line had been sold to a US trust in 1902, the younger Ismay
remained in charge, and keen to establish White Star at the
top.

Cunard's liners RMS Lusitania and RMS Mauretania were
taking more passengers on the trans-Atlantic routes, and they
were faster than ever before. They had both, separately,
earned the Blue Riband award for the fastest Atlantic
crossing by vessels of their kind. This was stiff competition.
So Ismay led with a vision of White Star being the most
successful passenger carrier covering the growing and
lucrative Atlantic routes. They were to distinguish
themselves on comfort, rather than speed.

White Star had a good record on comfort, showing
consideration for passengers in all classes. In many lines,
travel in steerage was unpleasant, even dangerous,
particularly for female passengers. US immigration agent

Anna Herkner travelled several times on different trans-Atlantic lines, investigating the conditions for steerage passengers. Here are some extracts from her report on steerage conditions:

"If the steerage passengers act like cattle at meals, it is undoubtedly because they are treated as such. The stewards complain that they crowd like swine, but unless each passenger seizes his pail when the bell rings announcing the meal and hurries for his share, he is very likely to be left without food. No time is wasted in the serving. One morning, wishing to see if it were possible for a woman to rise and dress without the presence of men onlookers, I watched and waited my chance. There was none until the breakfast bell rang, when all rushed off to the meal. I arose, dressed quickly, and hurried to the wash room. When I went for my breakfast, it was no longer being served. The steward asked why I hadn't come sooner saying, 'The bell rang at 5 minutes to 7, and now it is 20 after'. I suggested that twenty-five minutes wasn't a long time for serving 160 people, and also explained the real reason of my tardiness. He then said that under the circumstances I could still have some bread. However, he warned me not to use that excuse again. As long as no systematic order is observed in serving food in the steerage, the passengers will resort to the only effective method they know. Each will rush to get his share."

"Not one young woman in the steerage escaped attack. The writer herself was no exception. A hard, unexpected blow in the offender's face in the presence of a large crowd of men, an evident acquaintance with the stewardess, doctor, and other officers, general experience, and manner were all required to ward off further attacks. Some few of the women, perhaps, did not find these attentions so disagreeable; some resisted them for a time, then weakened; some fought with all their physical strength, which naturally was powerless

against a man's. Others were continually fleeing to escape. Two more refined and very determined Polish girls fought the men with pins and teeth, but even they weakened under this continued warfare and needed some moral support about the ninth day."

"The atmosphere was one of general lawlessness and total disrespect for women. It naturally demoralized the women themselves after a time. There was no one to whom they might appeal. Besides, most of them did not know the official language on the steamer, nor were they experienced enough to know they were entitled."

White Star was in certain contrast:

"The steerage ... presented practically no novelty and interest due to unique and inhuman accommodations. The same human needs were recognized as in the ease of cabin passengers, and every provision was made for these."

"The supervision ... was particularly strict; men were positively kept out of the women's quarters."

"There were four large dining rooms for the third class, two on the main deck and two on the deck below. Only the two on the main deck were needed on this trip, and even these were only about half full each. The one was used by the men passengers, the other by the women and families. The two were side by side and were served from one pantry, located between the two. There were long tables seating from ten to fourteen persons. At meals these were covered with white cloths and each place was set with a thoroughly usable knife, fork, and spoon. Bread, salt, pepper, and mustard were set till along the center of the table. Soup and meat were served from the pantry. Vegetables, preserves, pickles, and sugar were placed at either end of the table in large dishes and

3

each passenger could serve himself. Each table was in charge of one steward, who laid the cover, served, and attended to the wants of those there seated. The service and attention were real and all that could be asked. The food was all of a very fair quality and abundant. Absolutely everything served was such as might be eaten without hesitation by anyone. The preserves served with each breakfast and the fresh fruits, apples, and oranges given out several times at dinner were of an exceptional quality and would have made endurable meals of a much poorer quality. Coffee, tea, and hot water could be had by women and children at almost all hours of the day from the pantry."

The White Star service was clearly superior. High standards were set and met, so, when commissioning new liners, these were never going to be anything other than the best.

White Star Line was tied into Harland & Wolff, and could only go to them to have their ships built; in turn, Harland & Wolff could not build for White Star's rivals. Many of the directors of each company sat on the board of the other. They were a complementary partnership, and their fortunes were linked. Together, Ismay and William Pirrie, chairman of Harland & Wolff, had a vision of the Olympic class liners, with unprecedented luxuries, such as swimming pools and Turkish baths. This vision was first sketched out on a napkin, at a party in Pirrie's house.

Tense times in Europe meant that the British government had an interest in having large ships available for use. To ensure Cunard remained in British ownership, the government loaned Cunard £2.6million to finance Lusitania and Mauretania. The company also received significant subsidies, and a lucrative Royal Mail contract.

White Star was well placed to raise finance, though. The line was owned by a US trust, International Navigation Company, which subsequently became the International Mercantile Marine Company (IMMC). Its principal was JP Morgan; his intention was to dominate North Atlantic shipping, by eliminating competition and then standardising travel and freight costs, inland and at sea. He was a leading banker, willing to invest in success. Three of these giant liners were commissioned. Olympic and Titanic were to be built almost simultaneously. The third liner, Gigantic (Britannic), was to be completed later, funded by income from the first two.

Harland & Wolff was a well respected shipbuilder, with a proud workforce. Over the years, they had been both reliable and innovative. For the first two Olympic class ships, they commissioned a massive twin gantry and slipway, and set about their ambitious construction.

The vision for excellence of service was in place. Finance was arranged. Design and construction were to be carried out by world class architects and shipbuilders, who were already trusted partners of White Star Line. In their quest to dominate the growing trans-Atlantic passenger transport market, Ismay, Morgan and Pirrie had started well.

☆☆☆

In his book "7 Habits of Highly Successful People", Stephen Covey devoted one of the early chapters to this point *"Begin with the end in mind"*. Any project or enterprise should be driven by an idea of what it will deliver. The idea will then be refined, and tested against the vision for the business and its strategy. The accompanying business case, which answers the question "why should we do this?", should also be prepared, refined, and tested as the project progresses.

In this case, IMMC had a vision of market dominance, taking a leap ahead of its competitors. The vision was to be made reality by the construction of three sister liners, unrivalled in size, capacity and comfort, and these standards guided the subsequent work. The idea was little more than a sketch, but it was written down, and had enough credibility and support to be taken to the next stages.

There were uncertainties, particularly around external events, but there are always uncertainties – it's just a matter of degree. In this case, there was the threat of war. This would make sea crossing more hazardous, and could cause the government to requisition some of the fleet. Having considered that risk, the ships were commissioned. Without them, the vision for the future would not be achieved.

Those involved were leaders in their own areas, and all brought important and unique offerings. Ismay had the running of the White Star Line, and Pirrie had the ability to deliver the new liners. Morgan had the money, and his interest went well beyond getting a cash return on investment. He had a bigger picture, involving his other transport interests. The team was strong, and their venture had got off to a good start.

People

Identifying key stakeholders; backgrounds, roles and expertise; outsourced services; the Board of Trade as regulator; identification and management of risk

It is interesting to note the personalities and backgrounds of those who were behind the construction and running of the Olympic class liners. The owners and managers were typically from influential families, but had proven themselves in their businesses as they rose to the top. These men were opinionated, and capable of influencing at national and international level.

Others had a stake in the operation, too, from the workers in Belfast, to the crews on the ships, and agents at the ports. Even civil servants, the Admiralty and the British government could influence outcomes, and be affected by the success or failure of this enterprise.

This chapter considers some of the key people and organisations involved in the construction and operation of Olympic and Titanic.

Bruce Ismay

Joseph Bruce Ismay was born in December 1862, eldest son of Thomas Ismay, founder of the White Star Line. He was educated at Elstree School, and in France, before working in his father's shipping business, Ismay, Imrie & Company. He later served as company agent for White Star Line in New York, and in 1891 he returned to England, and was made a partner in the business.

Thomas Ismay died some eight years later, and Bruce took over at Ismay, Imrie & Co. The firm thrived, and Ismay proved himself to be a formidable businessman. In 1901, following an approach by an American conglomerate, terms were agreed by which White Star Line would become part of the IMMC, headed by CA Griscom. Following pressure from White Star shareholders dissatisfied with Griscom's performance, Ismay succeeded him in 1904.

Ismay's obituary in The Times described him as:

[a man] "of striking personality and in any company arrested attention and dominated the scene. Those who knew him slightly found his personality overpowering and in consequence imagined him to be hard, but his friends knew this was but the outward veneer of a shy and highly sensitive nature, beneath which was hidden a depth of affection and understanding which is given to but few. Perhaps his outstanding characteristic was his deep feeling and sympathy for the 'underdog' and he was always anxious to help anyone in trouble."

"Another notable trait was an intense dislike of publicity which he would go to great lengths to avoid."

During his time as White Star's agent in New York, Ismay met William Randolph Hearst. Hearst was a newspaper magnate, and therefore both influential and powerful. Ismay disliked press attention, and he and Hearst fell out over Ismay's refusal to cooperate with the press. This was a relationship that would subsequently haunt Ismay, and affect the world's perception of him for many years.

Captain Edward John Smith

Edward John Smith was born in Hanley, in 1850. He earned his master certificate at the age of 24, allowing him to take to the ocean, joining the White Star Line in March 1880. There he served aboard the company's major liners to Australia and New York, and made his way through the ranks, and ships, including Adriatic, Celtic and Coptic, and Germanic.

During his time as captain of the Majestic, he was awarded the Transport Medal. He was also an honorary commander of the Royal Naval Reserve, and in 1910 he was awarded the Royal Distinction.

Smith encountered several maritime incidents:

- He was captain of the Germanic when, in February 1899, she capsized at her New York pier. This was caused by ice in her rigging and superstructure.
- He was also in command of RMS Olympic, during the collision with HMS Hawke in September 1911, covered in more detail later.
- In June 1911, while manoeuvring the Olympic to a New York pier, a New York tugboat was damaged by the thrust from one of her propellers.

Perhaps such incidents were inevitable for a man with so many years of service at sea, and considering the giant new machines which he commanded. Despite these incidents, he was trusted by the White Star management, and had a reputation as a "safe pair of hands" with passengers. In his book 'Titanic', published in May 1912, Filsom Young described Smith as a man *"to whom the night of the sea was like day, and the invisible tracks and roads of the Atlantic were as familiar as Fleet Street is to a Daily Telegraph reporter."*

Smith is commemorated by a plaque in Hanley Town Hall, and a statue in Lichfield. The sculpture was by Lady Kathleen Scott, widow of Captain Robert Falcon Scott, also known as "Scott of the Antarctic".

Other officers

Position	Name
Chief Officer	Wilde, Lieutenant Henry Tingle, RNR
First Officer	Murdoch, Lieutenant William McMaster, RNR
Second Officer	Lightoller, Sub-Lieutenant Charles Herbert, RNR
Third Officer	Pitman, Mr Herbert John
Fourth Officer	Boxhall, Sub-Lieutenant Joseph Groves, RNR
Fifth Officer	Lowe, Sub-Lieutenant Harold Godfrey, RNR
Sixth Officer	Moody, Mr James Paul

Thomas Andrews

Andrews was born in Belfast in 1873. His father was a local politician, and his maternal uncle was William Pirrie, the controlling partner in Harland & Wolff. He became an apprentice at the shipyard when he was 16, and worked his way up to the role of director. He was also involved in the design, and was responsible for the final fit-out of the Olympic and Titanic.

Andrews was regarded as a family man, known to speak frequently of his wife and daughter. He was well liked, and trusted amongst the people at Harland & Wolff, and in the crew of White Star Line. He was approachable, and cared for his colleagues. Quarrelling stewards and stewardesses had been known to ask him to intervene, and William Murdoch, who subsequently became Titanic's First Officer, sought his advice on promotion. He also aided in the rescue of a man who had been trapped on an 80 ft scaffold by high winds.

His brother, John, served as Prime Minister of Northern Ireland; his other brother, James, served as Lord Chief Justice of Northern Ireland.

Alexander Carlisle

Born at Ballymena, County Antrim, on 8 July 1854, Carlisle attended the Royal Academical Institution, Belfast, of which his father was headmaster. At the age of 16 he was apprenticed to Harland & Wolff, through which he rose, and held various positions, including chief draughtsman, under-manager, shipyard manager, and general manager of the whole business, as well as chairman of the board of directors. He retired from these latter two roles in 1910, aged 56, and was succeeded by Andrews. Carlisle's brother-in-law was William Pirrie, the controlling partner in Harland & Wolff, and Andrews' uncle.

Carlisle was a passionate man, with strong convictions, and a member of the Privy Council. On one occasion he addressed the House of Lords from the steps of the Throne, and was subsequently reprimanded by the then Lord Chamberlain.

He was head designer in Harland & Wolff when the Olympic and Titanic were ordered, responsible for coordinating the designs; his main areas of involvement were the fitting out and equipment used on the ships.

William James Pirrie

William Pirrie was born in Canada. His parents returned to Ireland when he was 2 years old. He had joined Harland & Wolff as a "gentleman apprentice" in 1862, becoming a partner 12 years later. On the death of Harland, Pirrie became chairman of the company which employed 15,000 people. He was ennobled as Baron Pirrie in 1906, knighted in 1908 and made Viscount Pirrie in 1921.

Pirrie came up with the initial design of the Olympic class liners, in that he specified the length, the breadth, the depth, and the modeling. He started this in 1907, with Bruce Ismay.

He was well respected, and hugely influential in the creation and running of the Olympic class liners. Pirrie owned the second largest stock in White Star Line (after Thomas Ismay), and he was the main driver behind the sale to International Navigation Company, proving to be an astute negotiator in the deal.

JP Morgan

John Pierpont (JP) Morgan was born in 1837, in Connecticut. Following his university education, he went to Europe, becoming fluent in French & German. His banking career started in London in 1857, and he moved to New York a year later. During the American Civil War he was required, by law, to serve in the army, or to provide a substitute; he paid $300 for a substitute.

Morgan owned US Steel, General Electric and numerous banks and other financial institutions. As well as being a financier, Morgan made his wealth by acquiring struggling businesses, and returning them to profitability. His reputation was such that even the fact of his involvement in the business contributed greatly to the sale price when he disposed of those businesses.

He owned most of IMMC, effectively controlling White Star Line, Red Star Line, Dominion Line, American Transport Line, and the Leyland Line. The ships of these lines were under British registry with British crews. This was to avoid violation of the Sherman Anti-Trust Act of 1890, which regulated competition in the US.

In summary, Morgan was one of the most influential businessmen of his time. He, Ismay and Pirrie chose to work together, and, by any standard, would have been a formidable alliance.

The Marconi radio officers

The onboard radio officers were Harold Bride (21) and John (Jack) Phillips (25). They operated Titanic's Marconi wireless equipment, which was the most advanced of its time. Their duties were to handle normal maritime messaging, but also passenger messages for revenue.

Bride was born in London. After primary school he worked in the family business, to help pay for his training as a radio operator. He completed his training in 1911, and worked on several ships before assignment to Titanic.

Phillips was the senior radio officer. He was born in Surrey, England, and learned telegraphy while working in the Post

Office. He subsequently learned wireless telegraphy with Marconi, completing his training in 1906.

The equipment used a 4 wire antenna between the ship's masts, 250 ft above the sea. The main transmitter was housed in what was called the "Silent Room", next door to the operating room, and insulated to reduce interference to the main receiver. The working range was 250 miles, but communications could be maintained for more ‒up to 400 miles during daylight; much more, perhaps 2,000 miles, at night.

Titanic's callsign was MGY. Marconi was the dominant provider of radio services, and allocated their own callsigns, usually beginning with the letter M. Although by 1912 it had been replaced by SOS as the international distress signal, the distress signal CQD was still in common use.

The Board of Trade

The Board of Trade was the regulator. In this context, its role was to ensure compliance with the Merchant Shipping Acts, and related regulations. At the time of the disaster, the President of the Board of Trade was Sydney Buxton.

The actual members of the Board of Trade were not maritime experts, but mainly privy councillors, and included the Archbishop of Canterbury. According to the Merchant Shipping Act 1854, the Board's maritime responsibilities included the following:

"The Board of Trade is to be the department to superintend all matters relating to Merchant Shipping, and is authorised to carry out and enforce the provisions of this Act."

"The Board of Trade will also issue the forms of instruments, books, and papers, required by this Act and is empowered to make from time to time any requisite alterations."

"All Consuls, Officers of Customs, Local Marine Boards, and Shipping Masters, are to make such returns and reports as the Board may direct, and Shipping Masters may be required to produce the official log books and other documents."

"Officials of the Board of Trade, Naval Officers, Consuls, and Officers of Customs, may inspect such documents, and may muster crews. The Board of Trade has also power to appoint Inspectors to report on various matters."

In other words, the Board regulated and monitored the conduct of shipping, the design and fitness of vessels, and their crews. The Board was responsible for specifying the safety parameters, such as construction, or lifeboat capacities. Board inspectors were tasked with ensuring adherence to the rules.

In the aftermath of the disaster, the UK inquiry was commissioned by the Board, and reported to the Board. It investigated many things, including failures of the Board, its systems, and its processes.

☆☆☆

Some of those involved with the Olympic class were there from the beginning through to the launch of (what became) HMHS Britannic. Then, and now, people's interests, roles and rights differed, as did their personalities. In any project, it is important to know who the main stakeholders are, as well as what their interests are, and how influential they might be. How do matters look to each of them? Have they split loyalties? How might they affect outcomes?

Ismay was effectively the project director, managing the money, and making decisions on designs and delivery. He had the business acumen and the personality to do this job well. Smith was a salaried seaman, on what was intended to be his last sailing before retirement. He was competent, and respected, and so given responsibility for the safe running of the Olympic, and subsequently the Titanic. His stake began before the ships were completing sea trials, as he prepared to assume command.

The architects Carlisle and Andrews, both related to Pirrie, were clearly influential. However, their designs had to be approved by White Star, in the form of Ismay. Ultimately, it is the client who has to make the decision, or approve the end product. All a supplier can do is present options, sometimes with recommendations. The right to decide, and the accompanying responsibilities, lie with the customer.

Bride and Phillips were employees of the Marconi Company, not White Star, and were responsible for sending and receiving passenger telegrams. They also covered communications with other vessels, but their success was measured on the commercial traffic.

The Board of Trade was somewhat anonymous, enforcing (outdated) regulations through its understaffed and overworked inspectors. The Board wished to see compliance with law and regulations, although it came in for some criticism from the chairman of the US Senate inquiry.

From a business perspective, an analysis of the stakeholders must be conducted several times, as this will often point to strengths, providing reassurance, or weaknesses, requiring attention. It is one of many critical aspects of formal risk management.

Design

Design principles and features; luxury and safety; isk and complacency

Decisions and compromises

RMS Titanic was designed to be the grandest, most luxurious, vessel in the world. Safety might be considered to be a by-product of such standards, but this proved not to be a safe assumption. Claims were allegedly made that the ship was "unsinkable". This was perpetuated by the media following the disaster, as it had an ironic appeal. Subsequently, it was established that it was never advertised as unsinkable, although those with a stake in the vessel had done little to dispel any growing myth of unsinkability.

In 1906, Captain Smith said of the Adriatic:

"I cannot imagine any condition which would cause a ship to founder. I cannot conceive of any vital disaster happening to this vessel. Modern shipbuilding has gone beyond that."

If that was his belief of a much smaller ship, and of modern ships in general, he is unlikely to have changed his mind as commander of the Olympic or Titanic.

As reports were coming in on 15 April, Philip AS Franklin, a vice president of White Star Line, said:

"We place absolute confidence in Titanic. We believe that the boat is unsinkable."

Even without such statements, the ship looked unsinkable; people wanted it to be unsinkable. How could something so big, so grand, so modern be at all vulnerable? According to Walter Lord, in his book 'The Night Lives On':

"The owners were lulled into complacency. This was because the ship looked safe. Her huge bulk, her tiers of decks rising one atop the other, her 29 boilers, her luxurious fittings – all seemed to spell "permanence." The appearance of safety was mistaken for safety itself."

In the rest of this chapter, I examine selected aspects of the design, the design process, including approval, and materials used. This is to show how decisions, although perhaps of little consequence on their own, can cause an accumulation of risk.

Lifeboats

In his early designs for the Titanic, Alexander Carlisle specified a capacity for davits capable of holding 64 lifeboats, which would have catered for more than the ship's actual passenger and crew capacity of 3,547.

Carlisle was over-ruled by Pirrie and Ismay, and it has been speculated that he resigned over this issue. This may be true, given Carlisle's passion and assertiveness, but it is nonetheless speculation.

Why was the lifeboat complement reduced? There were several reasons:

- To avoid cluttering the decks and promenade. If these areas were to be occupied by the wealthiest of passengers, their experience should not be compromised by unsightly lifeboats in an otherwise luxurious environment.

- To reduce the worries of passengers, and promote confidence. Even if the worst happened, such an impressive ship would be its own lifeboat. To have so many lifeboats on show would be a display of doubt by the Line.
- Costs were important, and there would have been a secondary, financial benefit in reduced lifeboat numbers.

The actual number of lifeboats carried was 20 –

2 wooden cutters (capacity 40),

14 wooden lifeboats (capacity 65), and

4 collapsible lifeboats (capacity 47).

This was little more than the minimum required by the Board of Trade at that time.

Grand staircase and dining room

In keeping with the vision of opulence and luxury, Ismay instructed that the staircase by which first class passengers would enter should be made larger and longer. The grand staircase descended five levels, from the boat deck, to the D deck, and continued as an ordinary stairway to more first class accommodation, starboard on E deck.

The dining room was enormous, and Ismay did not want this compromised by bulkhead walls. Nothing should interfere with the comfort and service available to first class passengers. The design was therefore amended, providing lower bulkheads.

Bulkheads

Bulkheads are like walls within a ship, designed to create compartments. If a ship is holed, and one or two compartments flood, the bulkheads prevent the remaining compartments from flooding, and allow the ship to remain afloat. The diagram on page 31 shows where the bulkheads were in the Titanic.

Ideally, the compartments should be watertight, enclosed on all six sides. For reasons of access, this was not considered practical on passenger ships. Rather than have passengers climb stairs to get over bulkheads, doors were inserted. Above the waterline, this was not considered much of an issue; below the waterline, it was crucial. The design therefore included hydraulic vertical doors, which could be lowered into place by a number of different methods. If they were to be activated, alarm bells would sound, warning crew members to make their escape to upper decks.

Note the waterline. The bulkheads were just 10 ft above the waterline. This was as high as they could be, due to the grand staircase, the dining room, and other first class accommodation. Thomas Andrews had originally specified that they go up as far as B deck.

They may have been 20 ft lower than Brunel provided in the design of Great Eastern, some 50 years earlier, but they exceeded the requirements of the Board of Trade.

Hull

Great Eastern had also featured a double-skinned hull – effectively a hull within a hull. It was an innovation, not compulsory at the time. Thomas Andrews had originally designed a double hull, but once again the design was changed. Titanic had a double bottom, but her fatal gash was at the side.

Rudder

The rudder has been described as Titanic's "Achilles Heel", although opinion is divided on this point. The Olympic class ships were fitted with tall, balanced rudders. The contention is that the rudder was simply not big enough for such a massive vessel, and that a bigger rudder would have enabled her to avoid the iceberg.

What was required by law was that the rudder be of an area between 1.5% and 5% of the hull's underwater profile; Titanic's was 1.9%. Was this an example of the designers skimping? EA Stokoe, in Reed's Naval Architecture for Marine Engineers, stated that

"rudder area for fast ships should be 1/60th [1.67%] of hull area, and for slow ships 1/70th [1.43%]"

so that would suggest skimping was unlikely. The tall rudder design appears to have been selected for best performance at the vessel's designed cruising speed; shorter, square rudders were more appropriate for low-speed manoeuvring.

It therefore seems that the rudder design was fine. Certainly, better steering would have made it easier to avoid the iceberg, but there were no competing pressures on the design. If the lifeboat numbers were reduced in exchange for less clutter, there was no equivalent trade-off on the rudder design. The choice that was made was one that allowed for best steering at cruising speed, and she was cruising at the time of the iceberg sighting.

Rivets

In 1997, Science Daily reported that "tests of steel from the Titanic reveal that the metal was much more brittle than modern steel but the best available at the time". In fairness to Harland & Wolff, they could hardly have done better than the best available. However, the rivets used were a different matter.

Each of the Olympic class liners required three million rivets. This demand was enough to cause shortages, and the shortages are alleged to have peaked during the construction of the Titanic. Harland & Wolff had to go beyond its normal suppliers, and to use smaller forges, with output of less reliable quality. This issue is covered further in the next chapter.

Steel rivets had been used by Cunard on the Lusitania some years earlier. Steel rivets were used across the central region of the hulls of Olympic and Titanic, but in the stern and bow, iron rivets were used. There are two possible reasons for this. Firstly, the British Board of Trade required that rivet steel be tested, but since 1901 no longer required that iron be tested. This could help reduce delays, where a delivery schedule is under pressure. Secondly, steel rivets were driven by a hydraulic riveter, mounted on the gigantic gantry; it is entirely possible that a centrally positioned hydraulic riveter would not reach the fore and aft sections of the boat.

When using iron, like most shipbuilders of the day, the company normally used No. 4 bar iron, known as "best-best". However, they ordered No. 3 bar iron, known as "best", for the Titanic. I used to think that the word "best" was an absolute term, until my research for this book. Perhaps those ordering the iron thought the same. Only best is good enough?

In a study by Dr Jennifer Hooper McCarty, the decision to use iron rivets, made from No. 3 (best) may have lost the Titanic some valuable time. The bow is where the iceberg struck. This is where the inferior rivets were. Six seams opened up in the ship's bow plates. In their book 'What Really Sank the Titanic', Dr Hooper McCarty and Dr Timothy Foecke contend that better rivets may have kept the plates intact for longer, allowing the ship to remain afloat longer, and resulting in fewer lives being lost.

This study is considered somewhat controversial, but the question remains – did a design decision relating to type, quality and location of materials reduce Titanic's safety?

Funnels

The Olympic class liners each used 29 boilers to power the engines. 24 of these were double ended, and 5 were smaller, single ended. The smoke and fumes needed to go somewhere, clear of the passengers and crew.

The design provided for three functioning funnels, raked back to provide a sleek profile. Funnel No. 4 did not carry fumes. It was included purely for aesthetic reasons, rather than functionality, or safety. Having four would set the Olympic class liners visibly ahead of their predecessors. Perhaps this was an aesthetic extravagance, or designed to enhance the image of superiority. It didn't jeopardise the safety of anyone on board, *unless* it was kept in at the expense of something else, such as quality iron for rivets, or lifeboats.

☆ ☆ ☆

The design stage for any new operation is very important. There needs to be a clear high level idea of what it will be, and this will be refined as one approaches greater levels of detail, and as the project progresses. Throughout that process, the directors need to be sure that the investment remains worthwhile.

Considering the design decisions made by White Star, it's easy to say "I would have done it differently", but consider the circumstances at the time. The main driver behind the Olympic class liners was to provide a service of the highest standards, and establish White Star as dominant in the trans-Atlantic market, perhaps even a monopoly. Amongst others, the pressures included matters such as:

- Time to market (this is one reason why Olympic and Titanic were built alongside each other – get the return on investment as soon as possible)
- Availability of skilled labour
- Availability of required materials in good time
- Costs

In the face of such pressures, designs get changed, and compromises are usually made. The leaders / directors / sponsors make decisions based on the best information they have at the time, balancing these commercial pressures. Failure to make a decision is a form of decision in itself.

Ismay and Pirrie, the men leading the commissioning, design and build of the Olympic class liners, were formidable in their own roles, and didn't shirk their decisions. Titanic was to be the largest moving man-made object ever built. There would inevitably be tensions in the attempt to balance luxury, time, cost and quality. They may not always have been right, but they did what they thought was right, and no one mentioned the piece by piece erosion of safety.

The lesson here is that there is usually a trade-off between different requirements, and a risk to making decisions under severe commercial pressure. A shop with limited space may have to abandon one type of stock in favour of another. Concerns over quality of materials could cause delay to delivery. At each of these stages, decisions need to be made concerning changes. Such decisions need to be made by the right people, at the right time, with the best information they can get on the available options.

The preface to this book mentions features of Brunel's design for the Great Eastern, designed 50 years earlier. Walter Lord, in his book 'The Night Lives On', summarised the demands and the compromises with reference to the same ship:

"Passengers demanded attention; stewards could serve them more easily if doors were cut in the watertight bulkheads. A grand staircase required a spacious opening at every level, making a watertight deck impossible.... Stokers could work more efficiently if longitudinal bulkheads were omitted... A double hull ate up valuable passenger & cargo space; a double bottom would be enough."

"One by one the safety precautions that marked the Great Eastern were chipped away in the interests of a more competitive ship. ... **When the "unsinkable" Titanic was**

completed in 1912, she matched the Great Eastern in only one respect: she, too, had 15 transverse bulkheads."

The following page shows a profile of RMS Titanic, highlighting the waterline, the bulkheads, and the location of the collision damage.

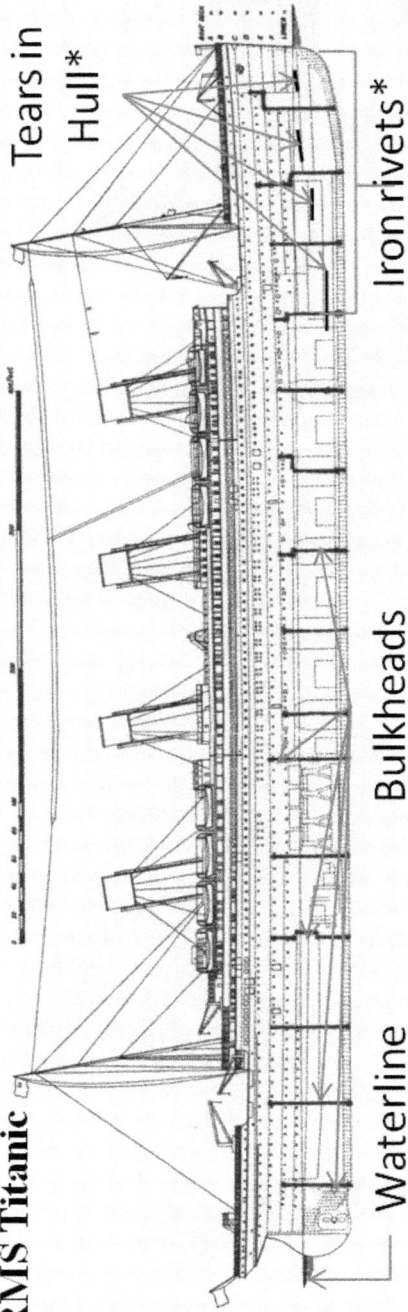

RMS Titanic

Tears in Hull*

Iron rivets*

Bulkheads

Waterline

* Approximate positions

Construction

Planning and delivering to schedule; equipment; materials; labour; finance; issues and impact; learning and adapting

"Perhaps the most remarkable of many remarkable things is the perfection of the establishment's organisation — no slight matter in an industry where the type of work is constantly changing, and where weights and measurements grow by leaps and bounds."

"All through this great shipyard, the biggest and finest and best established in the world, there is omnipresent evidence of genius and forethought; of experience and skill; of organisation complete and triumphant. In the doing of this great work—so various, so interdependent—all seems simple, whether it be in perfected details or vast combination. The building of a ship appears to be mere child's play."

**Bram Stoker, author of Dracula,
on visiting Harland & Wolff's Belfast shipyard**

The design of the Olympic class was followed by planning and construction of the first two vessels. When embarking on any project, it's usually a good idea to know, clearly, what is to be delivered. This is why design comes first, and can, of course, be refined. Planning follows, and involves breaking down the components of what is to be delivered (the liners), costing the materials and manpower required, and identifying when specific materials and skills are required. Next is *doing it.*

Construction wasn't limited to the ships. Other work had to take place to accommodate them. Southampton harbour had to be dredged to accommodate the deep draft of this new class; the Trafalgar dry dock had to be enlarged, as did the berthing piers in New York. Projects rarely deliver without external impact, and are always affected by external events and circumstances.

Directing and managing the liners' construction were done in accordance with established and maturing principles. Shipbuilding was an old trade, so methods could be repeated, and scaled if necessary. Governance was hierarchical, although there was plenty of robust discussion as the build progressed — this was no place for shrinking violets.

Schedule

The table below shows the main delivery dates for Olympic and Titanic, alongside other events that materially affected the delivery:

28 July 1908	Design plans for Olympic class ships approved in principle by White Star
31 July 1908	Contract signed for construction of three Olympic class liners
16 Dec. 1908	Olympic's keel laid
31 March 1909	Titanic's keel laid
20 October 1910	Olympic's hull launched
28–29 May 1911	Olympic's sea trials
31 May 1911	Titanic's hull launched
14 June 1911	Olympic's maiden voyage
July 1911	Titanic's maiden voyage date announced as 20 March 1912

20 Sept. 1911	Olympic and HMS Hawke collide, requiring 6 weeks for repair in Belfast
20 Nov. 1911	Olympic returned to service
January 1912	Lifeboats installed on Titanic
24 Feb. 1912	Propeller blade lost on Olympic
31 March 1912	Titanic completed
2 April 1912	Sea trials conducted; departed for Southampton
10 April 1912	Actual date of Titanic's maiden voyage, setting sail from Southampton

The two ships were being built just a few months apart. This was an aggressive and risky plan. A problem or delay with one could impact the other, but there were advantages to this approach. The date for Titanic's maiden voyage was set a few weeks after Olympic's had actually happened. This makes sense, as Olympic was in service, and no longer under construction. Barring unforeseen events, the remaining construction of the Titanic was predictable with enough certainty to go public with a date, and set about selling tickets.

Equipment

The ships began their lives in an enormous steel gantry – the Arrol Gantry – above two new slipways, with concrete foundations nearly five feet deep. The gantry was 840 ft long, 228 ft tall and 240 ft wide. It was a scaffolding platform, and supported a crane, used to lift giant tools, such as the hydraulic riveter.

Although built for the Olympic class, the gantry remained in use until the 1960s, a good example of extracting value from previous projects.

Labour

During the construction of Olympic and Titanic, Harland & Wolff employed approximately 15,000 people. The staggered, parallel construction meant that specific skills used in certain stages of Olympic's construction would then be transferred to the equivalent work on Titanic. The requirements for specific skills could be predicted, and the peak requirements could be planned for. Meeting those requirements might have been more of a challenge. Over the years, Belfast's shipbuilding heritage had created a large pool of skilled and expert workers. Additionally, skilled workers could be recruited from Glasgow or Liverpool, in many cases tempted by the promise of longer periods of work.

Materials

Rivets, mentioned in the previous chapter, became an issue, but not the only one. According to Dr Jennifer Hooper McCarty

"The board was in crisis mode ... In every meeting it was: 'There are problems with the rivets and we need to hire more people.'".

Her comments may be speculative, but they are plausible. As with labour, the requirements for construction materials were predictable. Each ship alone put pressure on the forges, and the supplies of coal and iron, for timely delivery. The construction of another ship of equal enormity exacerbated this.

Other factors to be considered about the rivets were the equipment used, and its access to certain parts of the boat. Where the hydraulic riveter could reach, steel rivets were used; where it could not, and they had to be driven manually, wrought-iron rivets were used. This would have happened regardless of any speculation about the quality of materials.

Finance

Lord Pirrie of Harland & Wolff was inclined to keep financial details to himself, which can be very frustrating. In any event, JP Morgan may have provided the bulk of the finance, but this was effectively within the charge of Ismay. Compared to Lord Pirrie of Harland & Wolff, Bruce Ismay had a very open approach to finances, and 'he who holds the purse strings calls the shots'.

White Star's close reliance on Harland & Wolff, and their long established and largely trusted relationship, meant that for one to succeed, they both had to succeed. Harland & Wolff had no reason to cut corners – the agreement between them and White Star Line stated that "she will be built barring no expense". The cost for the first two ships was to be £3 million, with any extras to be contracted, subject to a 5% fee.

All the time, money was going out, to pay suppliers. As with so many projects, pressure to deliver on time grew and grew, even when things were going to plan. Harland & Wolff were world class, though. The management and the workforce were very capable.

Learning and adapting

There were many notable differences between Olympic and Titanic. Some were in the original designs, and other differences arose during construction and fitting. For example, Olympic was under-ventilated, so a large proportion of Titanic's fans were enlarged to address this. Also, promenade decks and dining facilities were reconfigured to maximise revenue, based on experience from the Olympic in operation.

Issue: HMS Hawke collision

Probably the biggest issues affecting the construction of the Titanic were Olympic's returns to Belfast for repairs. The first was following her collision with HMS Hawke, while under the command of Captain Smith. The repairs took 2 months. The second, 3 months later, followed an incident where she lost a propeller blade.

The Titanic's delivery schedule suffered as a result of the Olympic's problems. Titanic had to be moved from dry dock, to make way for her sister. The impact was over 2 months, and it diverted resource and effort from Titanic. Titanic's maiden voyage was deferred for only 3 weeks.

Capability

As a project, the construction of the first two Olympic class liners was fairly typical. Design was refined, special facilities were created, procurement had some challenges, and skills needed to be balanced. Unpredicted incidents had an impact on delivery, which, in turn, was delayed. Overall, though, construction was conducted to the standard one would expect of Harland & Wolff, based on their record and reputation.

☆☆☆

Planning is important – project planning, business planning, capacity planning and more – these are all essential in a well run business. A project schedule will detail what is going to be delivered when, and what tasks need to be completed to ensure delivery. It will also inform what materials are required, and by when, so that orders can be placed, and stocks monitored. From the project plan, staff numbers can be predicted, so that recruitment can happen in time, and so that people can be redeployed when their jobs are done.

Cost must also be forecast. In scheduling the delivery, funding requirements can be estimated – how much is needed and when, so that drawdowns can be made from the banks or other sources of finance. In my experience, Ismay's more open approach is easier to work with than Pirrie's. Give a team or organisation as much information as they need in order to deliver smoothly. If planning is good, there should be no surprises, especially if information is shared freely.

Freely shared information has another benefit. Risk management usually focuses on identifying threats, and how to deal with them. A similar process applies to opportunities, which are more easily identified where there is a practical openness in the team / organisation.

Issues arise, and they need to be dealt with. In shipping, there is always a risk that a member of the fleet will be damaged and need attention. Olympic was seriously damaged and needed urgent attention. It had to be fixed, as a matter of urgency, as it was needed to earn vital revenues. The cost of the repair was more than just the labour, materials and facilities at Harland & Wolff. There was also the knock on effect on construction of the Titanic.

Perhaps Ismay demanded that Harland & Wolff repair the Olympic and keep the delivery of the Titanic to schedule, but redeploying people from one activity to another means that the first activity suffers. If you ask a busy team to do more, you must guide them in their priorities. The suppliers were willing to do their best, but there had to be limits. To contain the impact on Titanic to 3 weeks delay was probably quite good, in the circumstances, possibly due to some heroic efforts in Belfast.

The Bow of the "Hawke," the Damage being so Great That the Ram Has Been Mashed Flat

The Hole in the "Olympic," the Damage Below the Waterline being Much Greater Than That Above

RMS Olympic and HMS Hawke following their collision (from "Popular Mechanics" Magazine December 1911)

Testing and Assurance

The importance of a thorough transition; learning from others; sea trials and drills; compliance with regulation

Most working components of the ships were tested or inspected around their installation – plumbing, electrics etc. This chapter focuses mainly on the transition from fitting at Belfast to full operation, and the approvals by the Board of Trade – the body that needed to be satisfied that the ship was seaworthy, and could safely carry passengers.

Transition

A piano can produce music, but it needs a pianist to make it do so. Similarly, there is a difference between declaring that equipment can do what it is designed to do, and proving that those who operate it can make it work when the need arises.

In business change, the changeover (or transition) is sometimes under-addressed. This is frequently due to costs and time pressures. In my research, I have found nothing to suggest that time pressures compromised crew training and drills, but some aspects of their training were inadequate. After all, Titanic's maiden voyage was delayed by 3 weeks, so this offered plenty of opportunity for crew to practise drills, and familiarise themselves with the ship, and their place in any safety drills.

Learning from RMS Olympic

On 2 May 1911, RMS Olympic underwent her basin trials, when the engines were turned for the first time; she began her 2 days of formal sea trials on 29 May 1911. On successful completion of these trials, Francis Carruthers, a

Board of Trade surveyor, issued a seaworthiness certificate, valid for one year. Under the command of Captain Smith, she then set sail for her home port of Liverpool, and onward to Southampton. During this journey, Captain Smith and his crew familiarised themselves further with their new charge, practising turns, and adjusting speed.

Olympic's maiden voyage made excellent time, marginally exceeding her expected speed of 21 knots. Ismay telegraphed Pirrie on arrival, stating "Olympic is a marvel, and has given unbounded satisfaction."

However, in New York, one of the tugs, OL Hallenbeck, was caught in suction from Olympic's propellers, was dragged towards the liner, and suffered significant damage to her stern frame. A lesson learnt, perhaps.

Olympic's return voyage again made excellent time. Ismay and the White Star management were now reassured that their passenger timetables could comfortably be met. Business requirements were being fulfilled, and the ship complied with the regulations. The Hallenbeck incident was a reminder that giant ships may create new challenges. This was further emphasised on 20 September, in Southampton.

In preparation for manoeuvring past the northeast coast of the Isle of Wight, Olympic was completing a reverse S-movement. At the same time, following much the same course, HMS Hawke, a British battle cruiser, came in alongside. There was some debate about what actually happened, but it seems that the Hawke, at 7,350 tons, was sucked towards Olympic, six times her weight. Despite Olympic's attempt to swing away, Hawke struck her hard, creating a triangular hole, just between two of the watertight compartments. Captain Smith ordered that the watertight doors be shut, and knew that his ship would not sink.

Despite the major disruption to Olympic's schedule, and the knock on effects on Titanic's maiden voyage, there was a silver lining to this cloud. Probably the worst conceivable damage to this class of liner was to be holed at the waterline, where two watertight compartments met.

The first Olympic class liner had suffered severe damage, and had survived. No lives were lost, and there were no major injuries. The 1,300 passengers were offloaded. The cost of this lesson was a commercial nuisance, but it certainly boosted the confidence in the design and robustness of the class.

Guarantee group

There was a nine man "guarantee group" on board the Titanic, headed by Thomas Andrews. It was usual practice for any ship on its maiden voyage to carry a team of troubleshooters, to review her performance, report on areas needing attention, and, where practical, fix any snags they found. The name guarantee group conveyed a certain air of confidence – it suggested they were there to guarantee performance as expected, rather than troubleshoot or fix.

A place on the guarantee group was prestigious; to a member, it meant that Harland & Wolff had confidence in them, that they had made a favourable impression. Membership was a reward, and the prospect of membership an incentive to work hard and show commitment. Most travelled 2nd class, although William Parr, an electrician, and Roderick Chisholm, a draughtsman, travelled first class. Although they would have to work during the voyage, their accommodation was of an enviable standard of luxury.

The guarantee group's role was not so much testing as snagging, fine tuning, and assurance.

Titanic's sea trials

These were planned for 1 April, but delayed by a day, due to bad weather. As with Olympic, sea trials were required in order to get a certificate of seaworthiness. Titanic's sea trials lasted just half a day. The trials covered speeding up, turning at various speeds, and an emergency stop. The wireless equipment was tested and the lifeboats and their equipment checked – a further lifeboat test was to be carried out at Queenstown, before final Board of Trade clearance to sail, again granted by Francis Carruthers.

Lifeboat drills

The Board of Trade required that a lifeboat drill be performed at Southampton. This seems to have been considered a formality – checking that a sample of the davits were actually capable of being operated. Some crew members were put aboard two lifeboats, and lowered only part of the way down (two was the normal sample checked at the time). In summary, the drill was poorly executed, and wasn't completed. The test was inadequate.

Captain Maurice Clarke, an experienced Master Mariner and Officer of the Board of Trade, inspected Titanic at Southampton. Here is an extract from his testimony to the Board of Trade inquiry:

Have you any idea as to what would be an efficient method of drilling crews to man lifeboats in case of accident? - Yes; I think that all hands that form the crew should be exercised in handling the ship's boats, both firemen and stewards.

I take it that up to the time of the Titanic disaster that had not been the practice?

- Not in the White Star Line.

Not in the White Star Line?

- No.

A point to consider here is whether this failure was one of regulation, or common sense by White Star, and some other lines. In subsequent questioning, Captain Clarke was asked:

Is it not a Rule in other companies that the whole of the three departments – the deck, the steward, and stokehold departments take part in the boat drill?

- Yes, in some of the companies they do, and the men like it.

The regulator's inspector performed minimal checking, but acknowledged that the requirements were inadequate, and that he had an opinion of a better way to drill crews.

White Star ships typically conducted boat drills on Sunday mornings. All passengers, hands and crew would assemble at their respective boat stations. On Sunday 14 April, however, there was no such drill, and there is no record of why. Perhaps it was because there was believed to be no need, or perhaps it was because it would draw attention to the actual numbers of lifeboats.

General safety

Captain Clarke also gave evidence concerning the emergency doors leading from third class quarters to the boat decks. Many of the doors granting access were locked shut.

So far as you know, when she left were these doors locked?
- No doubt some of them were, but those are only emergency doors that are locked, not the doors to the third class passengers.

Quite; that is the emergency doors that led to the boat deck?

- Yes. Would you like to know the reason?

I do not mind?

- Well, the reason for having those doors locked is to keep the firemen and stewards and other people from passing through into the different places on sailing day. They are very congested. The ship is very congested from a lot of visitors - something like a thousand visitors.

This was common enough practice at the time, to control traffic of passengers and crew. However, a modern equivalent would be the locking of fire exits in a public building

The regulator's capacity

The Board's officers were tasked with surveying ships. The market was growing, as was the size of many of the vessels in this busy port. As often happens, the numbers of people employed to enforce regulations did not grow proportionately. Two further extracts from the questioning of Captain Clarke:

Will you answer a simple question? Are there enough Surveyors in your opinion?

- No.

That is an answer. Have you ever represented to the Board of Trade that there are not?

- That would not be in my province.

Have you ever represented it?

- No.

Let me tell you in my opinion, if that was your view, it was your duty to say so?

- I should get a very severe snub if I did.

Is there, in your opinion, in any branch of the service of the Board of Trade a sufficient number of men, in the opinion of the men who are in that service?

- No, none of us think that.

No, I am sure you do not; you all think there ought to be more?

- Yes, undoubtedly.

How many more; would you say double?

- Well, it is getting on for that.

Or perhaps treble?

- Oh, no.

Well, double; the whole staff of the Board of Trade, in your opinion, ought to be doubled?

- I think so.

Shortly after this exchange, the Commissioner of the inquiry added:

"I have no doubt they will have a great deal more work to do after the Titanic."

The regulator's processes

In any testing or checking, there is an element of box ticking. Lists are compiled and used to ensure that nothing is overlooked. However, there can be a tendency simply to apply those checks, without thinking about their overall purpose. This was made clear in the further questioning of Captain Clarke, who was prompted to become quite frank in his responses:

Then you do not think your system before this disaster was satisfactory?

- No, not very satisfactory.

Well, was it satisfactory?

- Well, I think we might with advantage –

Will you answer the question; was it satisfactory?

- No.

It was your plan, nevertheless?

- My plan? No, it is the custom.

Never mind about the custom; it is what you did?

- Yes.

And you now do not think it is satisfactory?

- No.

Did you think it satisfactory before the Titanic accident?

- Well, no.

Then why did you do it?

- Because it is the custom.

But do you follow custom, although it is bad? - Well, you will remember I am a Civil servant. Custom guides us a good bit.

This demonstrates something not unique to the civil service. In any business or operation, there is a need for processes and systems (custom) in order to operate efficiently. In this case, the processes were in place to inspect the adequacy of safety provision, but the processes themselves were known to be inadequate. Staffing levels meant that inspectors could do little more than apply their processes, rather than improve them. In any event, culture at the time discouraged people from speaking up where they had concerns.

☆☆☆

Senator Smith, convenor of the US inquiry, had this to say:

"Builders of renown had launched her on the billows with confident assurance of her strength, while every port rang with praise for their achievement; shipbuilding to them was both a science and a religion; parent ships and sister ships had easily withstood the waves, while the mark of their hammer was all that was needed to give assurance of the high quality of the work. In the construction of the Titanic no limit of cost circumscribed their endeavor, and when this vessel took its place at the head of the line every modern improvement in shipbuilding was supposed to have been realized; so confident were they that both owner and builder were eager to go upon the trial trip; no sufficient tests were made of boilers or bulkheads or gearing or equipment, and no life-saving or signal devices were reviewed; officers and crew were strangers to one another and passengers to both; neither was familiar with the vessel or its implements or tools; no drill or station practice or helpful discipline disturbed the tranquility of that voyage, and when the crisis came a state of absolute unpreparedness stupefied both passengers and crew, and in their despair the ship went down."

The term "quality management" may not have been in common use in the early twentieth century, but testing certainly took place, in order to ensure that what was being delivered was fit for purpose, and didn't fall foul of the laws governing operations. Was it enough?

The quote from Captain Clarke – *"custom guides us a good bit"* indicates an attitude that is still too often encountered, and not unique to civil servants. I am a big fan of process and systems, but only so long as they are good. Where they become box-ticking exercises, they can undermine their purpose. Consider this question – did the check take place so that the paperwork could be completed, or was it intended to demonstrate that any sample of seamen could operate the safety procedures efficiently, under pressure?

Perhaps it was arrogance, but it is clear that White Star Line did not countenance an event which would cause Titanic to require a full evacuation, at speed. The lifeboat drills, and the ability of the crew to complete them, were therefore little more than lip service to their real purpose – disaster recovery. Disaster recovery planning – procedures for recovery or continuation of core activities (in this case, the safe transport of passengers) – failed that night. A disaster for a modern business could be a fire, an explosion, or something else that prevents access either to a place of work, or to core systems, or prevents business from being carried out. A disaster recovery plan is needed, specifying how operations can continue, communication arrangements, responsibilities, and alternative locations for certain activities.

Some organisations are better prepared for disasters or emergencies than others. In my experience, businesses in Belfast were better prepared than most, not because of any Titanic legacy, but because of frequent bombings during the Troubles. Business owners and managers were all too well aware of the chance that a bomb could prevent them from carrying on business as usual.

Whether required by law, or not, all crew and seamen should have been capable of participating in the drills. The point for other organisations is this: just because you've met the legal requirements, it doesn't mean you're good. There is no badge of honour for achieving the minimum – it doesn't serve a business well to scrape by – all it does is keep the police, the tax authorities, the financial regulators, health & safety or others off your back.

Lowering lifeboats was difficult, but this makes it more important to be able to do it right, and quickly. A parallel can be drawn with the opening of Terminal 5 at London's Heathrow Airport in 2008. An excellent construction project delivered on time and under budget, but the transition was a disaster. Staff were inadequately trained, and unfamiliar with the layout and the systems. When put to the test, it all failed. This wasn't the fault of the staff, it was the fault of the people who planned and financed the transition, and who hoped that "It'll be alright on the night."

Learning from the Olympic's Hawke incident was understandable, but in retrospect, any reassurance taken from it was misplaced. Being holed in one place, but damaging two compartments was nearly the worst conceivable damage, and she survived. How many business owners or managers have sighed with relief, and thought "we got away with it that time". That's a sign that they might not be so lucky next time, and should therefore plan to prevent it, or mitigate the effects if something similar happens.

Communications and Information

What was known in advance; early warnings; internal and external communications

"The single biggest problem in communication is the illusion that it has taken place."

George Bernard Shaw

"Only in the Marconi room was the monotony varied, for something had gone wrong with the delicate electrical apparatus, and the wireless voice was silent; and throughout the morning and afternoon, for seven hours, Phillips and Bride were hard at work testing and searching for the little fault that had cut them off from the world of voices. And at last they found it, and the whining and buzzing began again. But it told them nothing new; only the same story, whispered this time from the Californian— the story of ice."

Filsom Young, "Titanic", published May 1912

Iceberg season

There is a season for icebergs, and 1912 was a heavy year for them. On average, just under 500 icebergs enter the shipping lanes; in 1912 approximately 1,000 did so. The Labrador Current, a cold current which encourages icebergs down "iceberg alley", had come much further south than usual that year. A report published in 2012 by Donald Olson of Texas State University-San Marcos suggests that this may have been influenced by the position of the moon, the closest it had been in 1,100 years, combined with a high tide. It had also been a mild winter.

Regardless of the cause, the presence of icebergs was known, warnings were issued in maritime journals, and ships were already making allowances for them in their navigations. Nonetheless, on 11 April, French steamship Niagara had been holed by a bump with two small icebergs. Carmania had travelled to her aid, although that was ultimately not required, and encountered the same ice field, reporting some of the icebergs as 250 ft high.

Temperature checks

A practice, common at the time, was to take samples of the sea water, and check the temperature. This was to serve as an early warning for ice. It was usually done by lowering a leather pouch to the water. The pouch had a streamlined shape, which reduced the risk of it pulling the control line through the hands of the seaman gathering the sample. However, Robert Hichens, who had been tasked with this duty, didn't have such a pouch, so he improvised, using instead an old, small paint tin. This may not have been fit for purpose; according to the affidavit of Mrs Mahala Douglas, provided to the US Senate inquiry,

"we saw a seaman taking the temperature of the water. The deck seemed so high above the sea I was interested to know if the tiny pail could reach it. There was quite a breeze, and although the pail was weighted, it did not. This I watched from the open window of the covered deck. Drawing up the pail the seaman filled it with water from the stand pipe, placed the thermometer in it, and went with it to the officer in charge."

It seems that the test process failed, and the results were sought elsewhere, so that the records could be updated. This was probably an insignificant matter, but it does illustrate that people can and do work around processes and controls, to give the impression of doing their job. The temperature test process was not a major control. In Robert Hichens' words:

"We had to do this duty every two hours. The quartermaster was standing by. After that we don't take no notice of it. We write it down in the log book for the junior officer, and it is copied off in the quartermaster's log book."

The look-out and the binoculars

Over the years, there has been some controversy over the supply of binoculars to the look-out. It has been rumoured that they were forgotten, or locked away, and that the officers wouldn't contemplate lending their own look-out glasses to ordinary seamen. This is all either untrue, or irrelevant.

Normal practice at the time was for binoculars to be carried by the officer of the watch (First, Second or Third Officer), but not the look-out man. In the British inquiry, Captain Bertram Hayes of the Adriatic was asked why. He replied:

-They are a source of danger, Sir. They spoil the look-out.

How is that?

-The look-out man when he sees a light if he has glasses is more liable to look at it and see what kind of a ship it is. That is the officer's business. The look-out man's business is to look out for other lights.

Similarly, when questioned about whether the look-outs would have identified the iceberg sooner, if they had binoculars, Second Officer Lightoller responded:

He might be able to identify it, but we do not wish him to identify it. All we want him to do is to strike the bells.

Ernest Shackleton, the famous Antarctic explorer, had also been called to testify at the inquiry, because of his knowledge and experience of ice. Of look-out glasses, he said:

- My Lord, I do not believe in any look-out man having glasses at all. I only believe in the Officer using them, and then only when something has been reported in a certain quarter or certain place on the bow.

- Yes, you have the whole range of the horizon in one moment with your eyes and you localise it by using glasses.

In summary, information required by the bridge would not have been enhanced by the look-out having binoculars. The look-out's role and method of communication were clear – one gong if there was something to port, two bells starboard, and three bells if there was something ahead.

Marconi

The Marconi radio officers are mentioned in the chapter "People", but what was the function of the Marconi room, and where did its officers fit in the crew hierarchy? The Marconi room and its officers provided an outsourced service. Bride and Phillips were employees of Marconi, not of White Star; at sea, they took orders from no one but the Captain. Marconi's money was to be made from the transmission of passenger messages.

Passengers wishing to send messages would go to the purser's office, where they would be handed a telegram form for completion. The purser would charge the passenger, and, ultimately, the Marconi Company would be paid. The form would be sent by pneumatic tube to the Marconi room. By the time Titanic was within wireless reach of the mainland (at Cape Race), there was an accumulation of messages to be sent. It was around this time that ice warnings were also being received.

Here is an extract from the British inquiry, where Harold Bride was being questioned about messages from the Californian:

I think you stated it was about 3 o'clock in the afternoon on this Sunday when you heard the "Californian" message?

- I said 5.

You knew it was an ice message?

- Yes.

I think you stated to the Attorney-General that you were engaged in adding up your accounts?

- Yes.

And then you went on adding up your accounts, and paid no attention to this message?

- No.

Then some time afterwards, I forget whether you gave us the time, you happened to hear it repeated?

- Yes, that is correct.

Then you had not written it down when you heard it the first time?

- *No.*

You knew it was a message to the "Titanic"?

- *Yes.*

Reporting ice?

- *Yes.*

You did not write it down?

- *No.*

You took no notice of it at all, but went on adding up your accounts?

- *Yes.*

You happened to hear it repeated, did you say, a quarter of an hour or twenty minutes afterwards?

- *Yes.*

Are you sure about the time?

- *Yes.*

Had you finished your accounts by that time?

- *No.*

Were you still on your accounts?

- Yes.

The message was eventually passed to the bridge, but what this exchange suggests is that passenger telegrams were prioritised over incoming ice warnings, which were regarded almost casually. The radio officers were working hectically to clear the pile; after all, that was their job.

This may seem like a breakdown in important communications caused by split priorities, but is it? Are one or two ice warnings not enough? Maybe, but the operations of the radio officers suggest that it was unclear what messages should be reported to the bridge, and within what timescales. In the absence of clarity, perhaps they were making decisions on what information to pass on. The following extracts from the British inquiry casts some light on this point.

Charles Lightoller, Second Officer, explained how messages were routed or prioritised:

- It is customary for the message to be sent direct to the bridge. If addressed 'The Captain', or 'Captain Smith', it is delivered to Captain Smith personally, if he was in the quarters or about the bridge. If Captain Smith is not immediately get-at-able, if not in his room or on the bridge, it is then delivered to the senior Officer of the watch. Captain Smith's instructions were to open all telegrams and act on your own discretion.

In other words, all messages should reach the bridge; if addressed to the Captain, it should reach him, or, in his absence, the senior officer.

Under examination by the Attorney General, John B Ranson, master of the Baltic, was questioned about how ice warnings were relayed. This extract gives further insight into what messages might reach a ship's commander:

You said: "On Sunday, 14th April, reports were received by wireless from a number of steamships of having passed ice and bergs in positions varying from 49.9 W., to 50.20 W., on the outward Southern track"?

- Yes.

Was that right?

- They were not sent to me officially. The operator gets those, and he transmits those to the different ships as they are passing along. I get just a list. They were not official; they were simply sent by the different steamers as we passed to the operator, and he makes out a list of them and sends them to me. They are not signed at all by the Captains of the other ships; they were not official.

They were messages received from other ships to him to transmit?

- To transmit to me. He would send to me. They were from the operators, but they were not sent to me specially, except this "Athinai" - that was. That was an official message signed by the Commander.

The Marconi room was very busy with commercial radio traffic. Jack Phillips reacted tersely to one of Californian's ice warnings, with this infamous message:

"Shut up. Shut up. You're jamming my signal. I am busy. I am working Cape Race"

The following table lists five of the ice warnings received in the Marconi room:

Time	Source	Message
14 April 9.00am	*Caronia* (MSF) – Eastbound. The message was delivered to the bridge, and posted for officers.	'Captain, Titanic - West-bound steamers report bergs, growlers and field ice in 42° N, from 49° to 51° W, April 12th. Compliments, Barr'
14 April 1.42pm	*Baltic* (MBC) – Eastbound. Message delivered to Captain Smith while he was with Bruce Ismay. Ismay took the piece of paper, and later showed it to several passengers. Captain Smith later asked for its return, and it was posted in the chart room.	'Captain Smith, Titanic. Have had moderate variable winds and clear fine weather since leaving. Greek steamer Athenia reports passing icebergs and large quantities of field ice today in latitude 41° 51' N, longitude 49° 52' W. Wish you and Titanic all success. Commander.'
14 April 1.45pm	*Amerika* (DDR) - Private message to the US Hydrographic Office in Washington DC, overheard by *Titanic's* radio operators. It was not delivered to the bridge.	'Amerika passed two large icebergs in 41° 27' N, 50° 8' W on April 14.'

Time	Source	Message
14 April 7.30pm	*Californian* (MWL) - Message to the Antillian (MJL), overheard by *Titanic's* radio operators. Message was delivered by Bride to the bridge, while Captain Smith was dining.	'To Captain, Antillian: Six-thirty pm, apparent ship's time; latitude 42° 3' N, longitude 49° 9' W. Three large bergs 5 miles to the southward of us. Regards, Lord.'
14 April 9.40pm	*Mesaba* (MMU) - This message never reached the bridge. Harold Bride was sleeping, and Jack Phillips was busy on the key sending and receiving commercial traffic.	'From Mesaba to Titanic . In latitude 42° N to 41° 25', longitude 49° W to longitude 50° 30' W, saw much heavy pack ice and great number large icebergs, also field ice, weather good, clear.'

In his book "Titanic and Other Ships", Second Officer Lightoller highlights the non-receipt of the Mesaba message as the key failure:

"when standing with others on the upturned boat, Phillips explained when I said that I did not recollect any Mesaba report: "I just put the message under a paper weight at my elbow, just until I squared up what I was doing before sending it to the Bridge." **That delay proved fatal and was the main contributory cause to the loss of that magnificent ship and hundreds of lives.** *Had I as Officer of the Watch, or the Captain, become aware of the peril lying so close ahead and not instantly slowed down or stopped, we should have been guilty of culpable and criminal negligence."*

During the inquiry, it emerged that the Californian's radio officer listened as the Titanic talked to Cape Race up to a few minutes before the time of the accident, then he turned in for the night. The message from Phillips was less than helpful, given Titanic's later predicament, but Phillips and Bride were working diligently, performing their roles as expected. Those messages addressed to the Captain reached him; others were held by the radio operators. In accordance with practice at the time, there was nothing unusual about this.

What was unusual was that Captain Smith gave the written message from the Baltic to Bruce Ismay. Ismay is alleged to have shown the message to some passengers. Despite Ismay's position in White Star Line, Captain Smith was commander. The proper place for the message was with the officers at the bridge.

The warnings listed above all gave co-ordinates for the ice. At around 6:00pm, Captain Smith ordered an alteration of the ship's course, slightly to south and west of its normal course, to South 86 West true. Speed remained high, however, and increasing.

☆☆☆

For many years as a change manager, I have maintained that if communications are poor in any change project, the initiative is doomed. The same rule of thumb goes for operations. Good business decisions come from having good information, at the right time, in the hands of the right decision makers.

It appears that the radio operators passed on what they should have passed on, in accordance with standard practice, but were more casual about passing on unaddressed warnings, such as that from the Mesaba.

The Collision

Speed; the lookout and the bridge; the collision; evacuation
and rescue; heroics, loyalty and desparation

So far, I have addressed the design and build of Olympic and Titanic, and some operational matters on the Titanic. We know how this ends. This chapter considers what happened in the hours before and after the collision, and the decisions that were made contributing to the loss of life.

Why was Titanic travelling so fast, at night, in what became poor visibility? One possible reason is that the Captain believed the adjusted course would avoid the ice. It was also possible that the officers considered it safe to travel at near full speed, and that look-outs would provide sufficient warning of any hazards.

Speed: Ismay's influence

Bruce Ismay always put passenger comfort and convenience ahead of speed. To him, improved speed of crossing would be a bonus, as long as it had no adverse effect on passengers. It would obviously be good for his line's reputation if, on her maiden voyage, Titanic improved marginally on Olympic, which had herself broken new ground. However his views on speed were recorded in the summer of 1911, in correspondence where he was being asked to let Olympic sail faster, and arrive on Tuesday evenings.

"I am not favourably disposed to trying to land passengers on Tuesday afternoon, but if, after talking the matter over with Lord Pirrie, Captain Smith and Mr. Bell the consensus of opinion is in favour of this being done, you may rest

assured I will not allow my individual feeling to stand in the way."

A letter from Ismay to Captain Smith, concerning the Olympic, stated:

"We confirm the verbal instructions given to you at Southampton last week that it will be right for you to go full speed when on the short track, subject to your considering it prudent and in the interests of safe navigation to do so. This instruction applies to both eastbound and westbound voyages when on the short track."

Despite attempts to do so, the inquiries uncovered no evidence of Ismay attempting to subvert the Captain's authority, or instruct him in any way. The British Board of Trade inquiry concluded:

"Captain Smith was not fettered by any orders and to remain on the track should information as to position of ice make it in his opinion undesirable to adhere to it."

In the US, Senator Smith went further:

"I think the presence of Mr. Ismay and Mr. Andrews stimulated the ship to greater speed then it would have made under ordinary conditions, although I cannot fairly ascribe to either of them any instructions to this effect."

Speed: on the bridge

After leaving Queenstown, Titanic covered gradually more distance daily. She covered 464 miles on the first day, 519 on the second, and 546 the next. In the minutes before the collision she was making her maximum speed of the voyage, about 22 knots.

As far as the bridge was concerned, the most southerly ice was 41° 51' N. This information came from the Baltic, and the course, adjusted earlier by Captain Smith, took them south of this, by 8'. Perhaps this southerly adjustment was enough to comfort them that Titanic would miss the ice fields. However, Mesaba and Amerika, whose messages did not reach the bridge, reported ice as far south as 41° 25' N. Titanic was sailing north of this position.

The most easterly warned co-ordinate of ice was at 49° W, from the Caronia. The officers should have been expecting ice from 49° W, but encountered it later, at around 50° W. At the risk of stating the obvious, they should have slowed down sooner.

The following extracts from Second Officer Charles Lightoller's testimony at the US Senate inquiry give some insight into what the officers were thinking. He was being questioned by Senator Smith, who asked him about a conversation with Captain Smith, during his watch; Lightoller said:

-We spoke about the weather; calmness of the sea; the clearness; about the time we should be getting up toward the vicinity of the ice and how we should recognize it if we should see it - freshening up our minds as to the indications that ice gives of its proximity. We just conferred together, generally, for 25 minutes.

-Capt. Smith made a remark that if it was in a slight degree hazy there would be no doubt we should have to go very slowly.

Did you slow up?

-That I do not know, sir.

You would have known if it had been done, would you not, during your watch?

-Not necessarily so, sir.

Who would give the command?

-The commander would send orders down to the chief engineer to reduce her by so many revolutions.

Did you see anything of that kind done?

-No, sir; I did not see it on the bridge.

And the captain was on the bridge?

-Yes, sir.

Following further questions, Senator Smith asked whether Captain Smith had left the bridge:

-He left the bridge.

With any special injunction upon you?

-Yes, sir.

What did he say?

-"If in the slightest degree doubtful, let me know."

Lightoller handed over the watch to First Officer Murdoch about an hour after his conversation with Captain Smith, and Senator Smith asked about the exchange:

did you talk with Mr. Murdoch about the iceberg situation when you left the watch?

-No, sir.

Did he ask you anything about it?

-No, sir.

What was said between you?

-We remarked on the weather, about its being calm, clear. We remarked the distance we could see. We seemed to be able to see a long distance. Everything was very clear. We could see the stars setting down to the horizon.

The Captain was sensitive to the ice danger, enough to state that speed would need to be reduced if the weather turned hazy. He communicated this to the Second Officer, but this was not communicated on the next change of watch, between Lightoller and Murdoch. The night was clear, and 24 of the 29 boilers were in use. Maybe it was taken for granted that the senior officers would see that the ship was slowed down, in the event of haze; ultimately, the responsibility lay with the Captain.

The collision

On Sunday evening, 14 April, at 11.46pm ship's time, Fred Fleet, one of two look-outs, signalled the bridge with three gongs of the bell, then telephoned the officer of the watch, declaring *"Iceberg right ahead."*

First Officer Murdoch ordered the engines stopped, then reversed. He ordered Quartermaster Robert Hichens to put the helm *"hard-a-starboard"*. He then pulled the lever to close the doors to the watertight compartments. The ship veered slightly to port, trading a head-on collision for a strike along the starboard bow.

The impact was barely noticed by the passengers. In the bottom of the ship, it was a different experience. The rush of icy water sent the firemen in the forward-most boiler room running before the watertight doors shut. Captain Smith had come to the bridge, and ordered an inspection of the damage by Thomas Andrews.

There had been a series of gashes or tears for a length of about 250 ft, mainly in the area where iron rivets had been used, causing flooding in five of the so-called watertight compartments. The design was such that she could stay afloat with the first four flooded, but that was the limit.

As each compartment filled, the ship would dip further, filling the next compartment, and so on. Andrews estimated that they had an hour, perhaps a little more, before Titanic would sink. At around midnight, Captain Smith went to the wireless room and instructed Phillips to send the distress call, CQD.

Harold Bride later quipped to Phillips *"Send SOS, it's the new call, and it may be your last chance to send it."* This was a reference to changes to international radio distress messages. SOS had been around for a few years, although Marconi still used CQD.

Evacuation and rescue

According to Captain Lord, of the Californian, his ship was 19 miles away. Her radio officer had gone to bed after the abrupt message from Phillips. Some crew members noticed lights from a steamer, and observed rockets, but they didn't recognise the rockets as distress signals. No sounds were heard. Crew of the Titanic noticed a steamer in the distance, and tried to contact it by morse lamp, but there was no response. Other ships, including Olympic, some 500 miles away, picked up the radio distress signals, and made preparation to assist.

At 12:25am, Captain Smith ordered the lifeboats to be filled, and the first boat left twenty minutes after that, less than half full. Ninety five minutes later, most lifeboats had departed, and most could have accommodated many more. The table on the next page contains approximate numbers of passengers or crew carried in each lifeboat:

Time launched	Boat No.	Number aboard / Capacity
12:45	7	27/65
12:55	5	40/65
12:55	6	25/65
01:00	3	32-50/65
01:10	1	12/40
01:10	8	27/65
01:20	10	47-55/65
01:25	16	42/65
01:25	14	51/65
01:30	9	48-56/65
01:30	12	32/65
01:35	11	56-70/65
01:40	13	54-64/65
01:40	15	57/65
01:45	2	20/40
01:50	4	34/65
01:50	C	32-39/49
02:05	D	17/49
02:20	A	12-14
02:20	B	25-30

The shortage of lifeboats had catastrophic consequences, but the lack of drills and experience made matters far worse. Lowering lifeboats had never been easy, and Bruce Ismay had been assisting with the loading of lifeboats, when he became concerned that loading and lowering lifeboat number 5 was slow. He called "Lower away" to the seamen and supervising officer, and was immediately told off by the supervising officer.

By 02:05, most lifeboats were away, but about 1,500 people were still on board the foundering ship.

Heroics, loyalty and desperation

The distress calls continued throughout. At 2:10am, Captain Smith released the radio officers from their duties. Despite this, Phillips continued sending messages, until he and Bride were forced from the wireless room by water.

Phillips had been so focussed on his work, that he barely noticed when Bride strapped a lifebelt to him. Sometime later, another member of the crew attempted to steal the same lifebelt. In an interview with the New York Times, Bride said:

"As I looked out the door I saw a stoker, or somebody from below decks, leaning over Phillips from behind. Phillips was too busy to notice what the man was doing. The man was slipping the life belt off Phillips's back."

"The stoker was a big man, too. As you can see, I am very small. I don't know what it was I got hold of. I remembered in a flash the way Phillips had clung on –how I had to fix that life belt in place because he was too busy to do it. I knew that this man from below decks had his own life belt and should have known where to get it. I suddenly felt a passion not to let that man die a decent sailor's death. I wished he might have stretched rope or walked a plank. I did my duty. I hope I finished him. I don't know. We left him on the cabin floor of the wireless room and he was not moving"

Bride made it to one of the last lifeboats, Phillips didn't. Bride found himself in the water.

"I felt, after a little while, like sinking. I was very cold. I saw a boat of some kind near me and put all my strength into an effort to swim to it. It was hard work. I was all done [exhausted] when a hand reached out from the boat and

pulled me aboard. It was our same collapsible. The same crowd was on it."

"There was just room for me to roll on the edge. I lay there not caring what happened. Somebody sat on my legs. They were wedged in between slats and were being wrenched. I had not the heart to ask the man to move. It was a terrible sight all around – men swimming and sinking."

"I lay where I was, letting the man wrench my feet out of shape. Others came near. Nobody gave them a hand."

Despite his injuries, Bride was lucky, and was picked up by the Carpathia, along with the other survivors.

The Californian, which had been closer, and whose crew had observed distress signals, arrived later and continued the search for bodies. The US inquiry concluded:

"The committee is forced to the inevitable conclusion that the Californian... was nearer the Titanic than the 19 miles reported by her Captain, and that her officers and crew saw the distress signals of the Titanic and failed to respond to them in accordance with the dictates of humanity, international usage, and the requirements of law."

"In our opinion such conduct, whether arising from indifference or gross carelessness, is most reprehensible, and places upon the commander of the Californian a grave responsibility."

"Had assistance been promptly proffered, or had (the) wireless operator of the Californian remained a few minutes longer at his post on Sunday evening, that ship might have had the proud distinction of rescuing the lives of the passengers and crew of the Titanic."

Had the Californian observed *"the dictates of humanity, international usage, and the requirements of law"*, perhaps many more lives would have been saved. Sadly, this last line of support failed. This failure, on top of so many others, led to the enormous loss of life suffered that night. In contrast, Captain Rostron of the Carpathia was singled out for praise:

"The committee deems the course followed by Captain Rostron of the Carpathia as deserving of the highest praise and worthy of especial recognition. Captain Rostron fully realized all the risk involved. He doubled his lookouts, doubled his fireroom force, and notwithstanding such risk, pushed his ship at her very highest limit of speed through the many dangers of the night to the relief of the stricken vessel. His detailed instructions issued in anticipation of the rescue of the Titanic are a marvel of systematic preparation and completeness, evincing such solicitude as calls for the highest commendation."

☆☆☆

In business, as elsewhere, elements of success often depend on heroics from individuals – people going beyond what is expected of them, because their sense of duty is greater. I've seen this many times in both the private and public sector – targets being met because of the dedication of a few individuals, despite many challenges. In the case of the Titanic, we don't know how many extra lives were saved by the continued efforts of Bride and Phillips, or of crew and others who helped load the lifeboats.

Nor do we know how much more could have been achieved. How many people "gave up", resigned to their fate, or were so disparate that they tried to survive at the cost of others?

Despite circumstances, success is often delivered through the determination of team members, or threatened by the indifference of others. When recruiting staff, or defining a team, consider the emphasis on reliability and dedication. When the pressure's on, who will make a difference?

There is also a fundamental point to be observed about conscientiousness, and how people with defined roles understand those roles, and their overlap with others. In his conversation with Second Officer Lightoller, Captain Smith said "If in the slightest degree doubtful, let me know", but this does not appear to have been relayed to First Officer Murdoch. This leads to a question I struggle to answer – was Titanic's speed high because individual officers thought that *someone else* had decided that it was safe, and they were too polite or deferential to question the decision?

I don't know the answer, but consider this: should people, especially at a senior operational level, be empowered or even encouraged to raise concerns over operational decisions? Consider some of the world's biggest banks where lack of challenge, combined with inadequate audit and regulation, let major errors of judgement bring them down, and risk the economies of sovereign countries.

The principle can be scaled to smaller businesses, where the leadership should be open to challenge about risks they may not perceive fully. Take account of the icebergs, and adjust accordingly.

After the Disaster

The inquiries; Bruce Ismay; White Star Line; RMS Olympic;
HMHS Britannic

The inquiries

The British Board of Trade inquiry lasted 36 days, and heard from nearly 100 witnesses. The US Senate inquiry had to subpoena all surviving British crew and passengers while they were still in the US. The inquiry was led by Senator William Alden Smith, already an established campaigner on transport safety, and it lasted 18 days. The first witness called to testify was Bruce Ismay.

The main conclusions were similar, finding that the collision was caused by cruising at speed into a known danger area, that lifeboats were neither filled nor crewed properly, and that the Californian should have responded more quickly. The main recommendations were for more lifeboats, better drills, and continuous manning of wireless equipment on passenger ships. New regulations were proposed, requiring double hulls, and better bulkheads. The International Ice Patrol was established, and the International Convention for the Safety of Life at Sea (SoLaS) harmonised maritime safety regulations.

In answer to the question *"Did each boat carry its full load and, if not, why not?"* (question 20 (d) in the British inquiry) the answer was:

"At least 8 boats did not carry their full loads for the following reasons: -

Many people did not realise the danger or care to leave the ship at first.

Some boats were ordered to be lowered with an idea of then coming round to the gangway doors to complete loading.

The officers were not certain of the strength and capacity of the boats in all cases."

In other words, there was unpractised chaos.   On the subject of third class passengers, the inquiry reported:

"It is no doubt true that the proportion of third class passengers saved falls far short of the proportion of the first and second class, but this is accounted for by the greater reluctance of the third class passengers to leave the ship, by their unwillingness to part with their baggage, by the difficulty in getting them up from their quarters, which were at the extreme ends of the ship."

The British Board of Trade Inquiry omitted recommendations on weaknesses in its own administration from the final report, preferring to deal with them elsewhere. Senator Smith was more critical:

"We shall leave to the honest judgment of England its painstaking chastisement of the British Board of Trade, to whose laxity of regulation and hasty inspection the world is largely indebted for this awful fatality."

Ismay and White Star Line

After the disaster, Ismay was vilified by the press, especially papers run by William Randolph Hearst. As mentioned earlier, he and Ismay did not enjoy each other's company.

Hearst's papers referred to him as "J Brute Ismay", and one suggested that the emblem of the White Star Line should be changed to a "yellow liver". However, the documented testimonies don't support this portrait. Lord Mersey, in the British inquiry report, wrote:

"As to the attack on Mr. Bruce Ismay, it resolved itself into the suggestion that, occupying the position of Managing Director...some moral duty was imposed upon him to wait on board until the vessel foundered. I do not agree. Mr. Ismay, after rendering assistance to many passengers, found C collapsible, the last boat on the starboard side, actually being lowered. No other people were there at the time. There was room for him and he jumped in. Had he not jumped in he would merely have added one more life, namely, his own, to the number of those lost."

He may have been the president of the line, but he was a passenger, not a crew member. Even so, he helped time and again in the lowering of lifeboats. His "crime" was to have jumped into the last boat, where there was room.

Ismay maintained a low public profile, and retired to the west of Ireland in the mid 1920s, returning to England a decade later, where he died in 1937, aged 74.

White Star Line survived with a damaged reputation, and was purchased by the Royal Mail Steam Packet Company in 1927. That company was later liquidated, and its lines taken over by Royal Mail Lines Limited in 1932. In 1933, the British government rescued both Cunard and White Star, on the condition that they merged their North Atlantic operations, creating Cunard White Star in 1934. In the late 1940s, following further shifts in ownership, the "White Star" name was dropped. However, on RMS Queen Mary 2, MS Queen Victoria and MS Queen Elizabeth, Cunard introduced "White Star Service" as the name of the brand of services on those ships.

There were several more changes of ownership, and in 1998 Cunard was acquired by Carnival Corporation; Carnival later commissioned and owned the Costa Concordia which ran aground in January 2012.

RMS Olympic

Following her return to England, Olympic was hurriedly fitted with more lifeboats, all collapsible. As she prepared to depart Southampton later in April, her firemen went on strike, as they believed the lifeboats weren't seaworthy. The local White Star manager responded by saying that they had been declared seaworthy by a Board of Trade inspector.

To settle the matter, a test was done on four of the new lifeboats. One failed, so it was replaced. The firemen agreed to resume work on the condition that the strike-breakers were removed. On 4 May, the strikers were found guilty of mutiny in Portsmouth, but they were discharged without punishment, due to the circumstances. Olympic set sail on 15 May, with both strikers and strike-breakers aboard.

After extensive enhancement to bulkheads, the addition of an inner skin, and increased lifeboat numbers, Olympic continued in service as a passenger liner for several years. On 27 October 1914, she was involved in the rescue of HMS Audacious, taking on board 250 men, after Audacious had been hit by a mine. It was early in the First World War, and White Star intended to lay her up until circumstances changed. However, in 1915, she was requisitioned by the Admiralty for troop transport.

In May 1918, Olympic sighted U-boat U-103, which was preparing to fire on her. Her gunners opened fire, and she rammed the U-boat, causing the German crew to scuttle and abandon it. Two of Olympic's hull plates were dented, and her prow was twisted, but she was not breached.

In 1934, there was a further reminder of the power and control challenges of the Olympic class ships. In heavy fog, she struck the Nantucket Lightship, causing seven fatalities, from a crew of eleven.

The next year, she was sold for demolition, initially in Jarrow. Her final demolition took place in 1937, at TW Ward's yard in Inverkeithing, Scotland.

HMHS Britannic

Britannic, originally to be called "Gigantic", saw service as a hospital ship, having been requisitioned in November 1915. Her entry into commercial service had been prevented, due to the shipyard having to prioritise military vessels. One year later, she struck a mine and sank. 1,036 people were saved, 30 lost.

☆☆☆

The sinking of the Titanic was not the end of the story. Underwriters at Lloyd's of London took a hit, and White Star's reputation was damaged, but the company still survived. This was partly due to war - the British Admiralty needed ships and shipyards.

Lessons learned from Titanic were applied. Olympic's inner skin helped her survive the encounter with U-103. When Britannic sank, loss of life was 3%, not 68% when her sister went down.

Businesses come and go with the commercial realities of their time, changing hands, winding down, or shifting emphasis. The enterprise of shipbuilding was, and still is, a quest for improvement, combining efficient production with higher standards of functionality and safety. This aspiration is best summarised by a philosophy carved in a rock at the Newport News shipyard, where a great number of US ships were built:

"We shall build good ships here.
At a profit – if we can.
At a loss – if we must.
But always good ships."

The words came from elsewhere, but the approach would have been familiar to Ismay, Pirrie and Andrews – set high standards and meet them. Sadly, they were unaware of the effect that some decisions would have.

Conclusion

"It is a rash man indeed who would set himself up as the final arbiter on all that happened the incredible night the Titanic went down."

Walter Lord, author of "A Night to Remember"
& "The Night Lives on"

In concluding this book, I have to agree with Walter Lord. In the last 100 years there has been plenty of speculation and debate about why the disaster happened. Perhaps people's opinions are formed by the question asked in the first instance.

Any business enterprise should be driven by vision, and that vision supported by strategy, high standards, and efficient operations. Randomness plays a part in how things work out, but no one should rely on luck. Obstacles will arise, but the key is to know how to identify them in advance, and deal with them properly if they materialise.

To the question "why did Titanic sink?", the answer is "because she was travelling fast, on a moonless night, and hit an iceberg". I think a better question is "why were so many lives lost on Titanic's maiden voyage?". The answer to that question is touched on throughout this book, and it's a combination of design trade-offs, inadequate preparation for service, and poor communications. The White Star executives didn't question enough, and the passengers trusted both White Star and the Board of Trade's licensing standards.

There was no intentional erosion of safety, but there was arrogance and carelessness in White Star, and negligence on the part of the captain of the California. The loss of life was not caused by so-called "bad luck".

☆☆☆

In finishing, here is an extract from the final report of the British Board of Trade inquiry, followed by a self-explanatory graph.

> *25. When the Titanic left Queenstown on or about 11th April last was she properly constructed and adequately equipped as a passenger steamer and emigrant ship for the Atlantic service?*
>
> ***ANSWER:*** *Yes.*

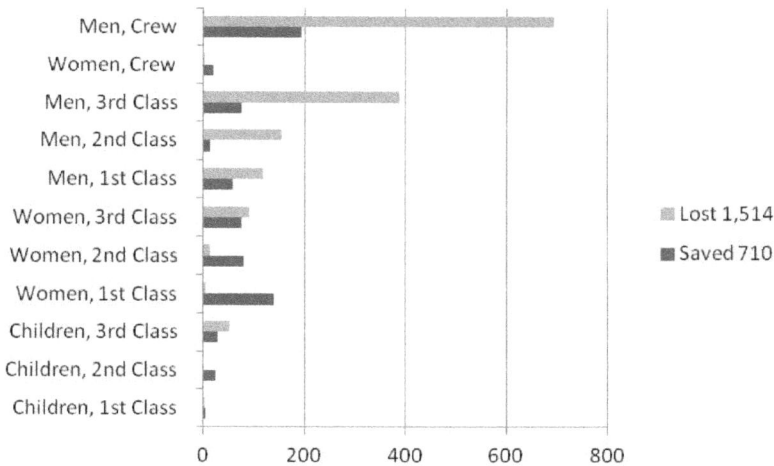

References

The following resources were used in my research for this book. Any quotes are noted within the text.

Books

Lord, Walter: *The Night Lives On* Thorndike Press 1986

Ballard, Dr Robert D: *The Discovery of the Titanic* Guild Publishing 1987

Kozak-Holland, Mark: *Titanic Lessons for IT Projects* Multi-Media Publications Inc 2005

Young, Filson: *Titanic* Chiswick Press 1912

Hooper McCarty, Dr Jennifer, and Foecke, Dr Timothy: *What Really Sank the Titanic* Citadel Press 2008

Lightoller, Charles Herbert: *Titanic and Other Ships* Ivor Nicholson and Watson, 1935

Newspapers

New York Times, 28 April 1912, *"Thrilling tale by Titanic's surviving wireless man"* (interview with Harold Bride)

New York Times, 15 April 2008, Broad, William J, *"In Weak Rivets, a Possible Key to Titanic's Doom"*

Web resources

Titanic Inquiry Project: www.titanicinquiry.org Transcripts of both the US Senate and British Board of Trade inquiries into the disaster

National Museums Northern Ireland: www.NMNI.com
History and photos of Olympic class ships

Encyclopaedia Titanica: www.encyclopedia-titanica.org
RMS Titanic history and facts

Titanic Titanic: www.titanic-titanic.com
Titanic information resources

BBC History: www.bbc.co.uk/history
Louden-Brown, Paul: "Titanic: Sinking the Myths"

Reports of the US Immigration Commission, Steerage conditions: www.archive.org

ABOUT THE AUTHOR

Kevin McPhillips is a freelance change management consultant, and has managed and consulted on change in a variety of organisations. These include PwC, IBM, Royal Bank of Scotland, Lloyds Banking Group, AEGON, and many government bodies, covering Health, Education, Employment, and Criminal Justice.

Kevin spent over 20 years as a keen skydiver, parachute instructor and coach, and attributes much of his attitude to managing risk to his skydiving experiences. He is also an experienced management trainer, a qualified hypnotherapist and a master practitioner of NLP (Neuro-Linguistic Programming), and has worked with Dale Carnegie© Training in the UK.

Having grown up in Ireland, Kevin now lives in Scotland with his wife, Marian, and children Conor, Iona and Tara.

ACKNOWLEDGMENTS

Special thanks to Brian Fitzearl, Peter Dalziel, Adam Pollock, Billy McKeown and Ian Kendall, who provoked my thoughts about RMS Titanic, usually making me laugh in the process, and to Andrew Hilton and Penny Smith, for their editorial advice.

www.ingramcontent.com/pod-product-compliance
Lightning Source LLC
Chambersburg PA
CBHW060634210326
41520CB00010B/1596